Dedication

Grateful for my family's unwavering support and love. You have been my rock and safe haven. Thank you for always being there. To God, I am humbled by your grace and guidance. Your love has been a constant presence in my life and I am forever grateful.

Contents

Chapter 1: Resilience

- Introduction to Anthony Eagle Jr.'s story of resilience
- Overcoming difficult circumstances and finding strength in adversity

Chapter 2: The Dark Days

- A mother's journey through her son's time in prison
- The turning point that led to Anthony's transformation

Chapter 3: The Healing Power of Writing Your Story

- The therapeutic impact of writing and storytelling
- Finding healing and hope through the power of words

Chapter 4: Lost and Found Through Addiction and Betrayal

- Struggling with addiction and the pain of betrayal
- Overcoming obstacles and learning to trust again

Chapter 5: Standing Up for What's Right

- Facing challenges and standing up for one's beliefs
- The importance of speaking up and taking action

Chapter 6: Struggling Through Pain

- Coping with physical and emotional pain
- Finding strength and support in difficult times

Chapter 7: The Realization

- Coming to terms with past mistakes and regrets
- Learning to forgive oneself and move forward

Chapter 8: Meet Mom and Dad

- The impact of family and positive role models
- Overcoming the odds with the help of loved ones

Chapter 9: Choices

- The power of choice and taking responsibility for one's actions
- Making positive changes and taking control of one's life

Chapter 10: Uncle No Name

- The impact of family dysfunction and addiction
- Finding hope and support in unexpected places

Chapter 11: Meet Jack

- The value of mentorship and guidance
- The impact of positive relationships on personal growth

Chapter 12: Bad Decisions

- Dealing with the consequences of poor decision-making
- Learning from mistakes and moving forward

Chapter 13: Breaking the Cycle

- Overcoming generational patterns and cycles of dysfunction
- Making positive changes for oneself and future generations

Chapter 14: Meet Kat

- The power of friendship and connection

- Finding support and encouragement through relationships

Chapter 15: The Big Move

- Making major life changes and taking risks

- The rewards of stepping outside of one's comfort zone

Chapter 16: Walk What We Talk

- Living in alignment with one's values and beliefs

- The journey of self-discovery and personal growth

"Broken, But Not Destroyed: A Kintsugi Journey to Resilience"

CHAPTER 1

The Japanese art form that uses broken ceramics, such as plates and bowls, and then mends them together using gold or silver lacquer is called "kintsugi" (金継ぎ), which translates to "golden joinery" or "golden repair." Kintsugi is a traditional Japanese technique that dates back to the 15th century and is often seen as a metaphor for embracing imperfection and finding beauty in the broken or flawed.

As a child growing up on a reservation, life was tough. We were poor and had to make do with what we had. My dad was in prison, and my mom struggled to provide for us. As the second oldest, I felt responsible for my siblings' well-being and safety. I was their protector.

When my dad was released from prison, I thought things would get better. But instead, he became more like a gang leader than a father. He showed me the negative aspects of life, teaching me how to sell drugs and how to be relentless in fights. He showed me how not to be a man, and I fell into a cycle of addiction by the age of 13.

My addiction to drugs continued to spiral out of control, and I found myself using heroin by the age of 15. Cocaine and other hard drugs became a weekly part of my life. I was no longer the protector of my family, but a shell of the person I once was. I carried doubt, dishonesty, lack of loyalty, and a lack of understanding for the people who loved me the most.

My days were filled with creating victims, and I didn't know how to break the cycle. The weight of the choices I made became heavy, and I knew that I needed to make a change.

This is my story, the story of a boy who grew up on a reservation, fell into the cycle of addiction, and struggled to break free. But I am also the story of a man who found redemption, who fought for his family, and who learned how to be a true protector.

When I was 14 years old, I had a traumatic experience that has stayed with me for a long time. I was at the park playing with my older brother Josh, who is 16 years old, when we got into a fight with another kid. I stepped in to protect my brother and ended up slamming the other kid to the ground. I was tempted to hit him, but I decided not to and walked away feeling proud of myself.

However, things took a dark turn when we got back to the house. My dad took my siblings out to buy them chips and soda, but he didn't get me anything. Instead, he said he had something special for me and took me down to the basement. He took out a rod from a tent and repeatedly hit me in the face and head about six times. It was a traumatizing experience that left me feeling scared, confused, and betrayed.

As I look back on that experience, I realize that my dad robbed me of my "fight or flight" response. Instead of feeling empowered to stand up for myself and others, I felt scared and helpless. It was a difficult and painful experience that has stayed with me for a long time.

It's important to remember that you're not alone. Many people have experienced trauma or abuse, and it's important to seek help and support to heal and recover.

One important step is to talk to a therapist or counselor. They can help you work through your feelings and experiences in a safe and supportive environment. They can also help you develop coping strategies for dealing with stress and anxiety.

It's also important to remember that healing takes time. It's okay to take things one step at a time and to be patient with yourself. You may need to work through difficult emotions and memories, but it's possible to overcome them with the right support.

In addition to therapy, there are other things you can do to take care of yourself. This might include practicing mindfulness or relaxation techniques, engaging in physical exercise or other activities that brings you joy, and surrounding yourself with supportive and caring people.

Remember that you deserve to feel safe, valued, and loved. You have the right to set boundaries and to stand up for yourself and others in healthy and productive ways. With time and effort, you can heal from the trauma and move forward towards a brighter future.

The Dark Days "Broken but not Destroyed" A Mother's Journey: How My Son's Time in Prison Became His Turning Point

Chapter 2

As a mother, it's hard to watch your child struggle. My son was no exception. He had a rough upbringing, filled with pain and struggle. He turned to drugs and alcohol to ease the pain, and before I knew it, he was a skid row junkie. I tried everything I could to help him, but nothing seemed to work.

One day, I got a call from the police. My son had been arrested for drug possession and was facing serious charges. I was devastated, but I knew that he needed help. He was sentenced to six years in prison, and that became a turning point for him.

At first, I was scared for him. I knew that prison was a dangerous place, and I worried about his safety. But as time went on, I started to see a change in him. He started to get his mind right, to focus on his future. He used his time in prison to reflect on his life and the mistakes he had made.

He talked to me about how he had always felt lost, like he had no direction in life. He had turned to drugs and alcohol to ease the pain, but it only made things worse. He realized that he needed to change his mindset, to believe in himself and his abilities. He started to read self-help books and to attend counseling sessions. He was determined to make a change.

Prison became his standstill, a place where he could focus solely on himself and his mental and emotional well-being. He used the time to get his mind right, to work on his personal growth, and to set goals for himself. He realized that he had a purpose in life, and that purpose was to help others.

As a family member of someone who is in prison, it's easy to feel helpless. But there are things you can do to support your loved one. Write them letters, send them books and magazines, and let them know that you love them and believe in them. Encourage them to use their time in prison to reflect on their life and to work on personal growth.

Formula for Getting Through the prison sentence:

If you or someone you love is struggling with addiction or facing time in prison, there is hope. Here are some things that helped my son get through the dark days:

<u>1. Acceptance: Accept that you have a problem and that you need help. You can't change the past, but you can change the future.</u>

<u>2. Mindset: Change your mindset. Believe in yourself and your abilities. Visualize your goals</u>

and dreams, and use positive affirmations to help you stay focused.

3. Personal Growth: Focus on personal growth. Read self-help books, attend counseling sessions, and work on setting goals for yourself.

4. Support: Surround yourself with positive influences. Seek out friends and family members who support you and encourage you to be your best self.

5. Purpose: Find your purpose. What is it that you're passionate about? How can you use your experiences to help others?

My son's time in prison was a difficult time for our family, but it also became his turning point. He used his time to reflect on his life, to work on personal growth, and to find his purpose. He is now a manifestation master, using his experiences to inspire hope and deliver options for ways out too

As my mother said, prison became my standstill. It was a place where I could focus on myself and my personal growth. I spent my days reading self-help books, attending counseling sessions, and setting goals for myself.

One of the most important things I learned during my time in prison was the power of manifestation. I started to visualize my goals and dreams, and I used positive affirmations to help me stay focused. I believed in myself and my abilities, and I knew that I could achieve success if I put in the work.

But it wasn't easy. Prison was a difficult place, filled with negativity and danger. I had to learn how to navigate the system, how to avoid trouble, and how to stay safe. I also had to deal with the emotional toll of being separated from my family and friends.

But through it all, I remained focused on my personal growth. I knew that I had a purpose in life, and that purpose was to help others. I wanted to use my experiences to inspire hope and deliver options for ways out to others who were struggling with addiction or facing time in prison.

The Road to Recovery

After six years in prison, which wouldn't be my last. I was released. It was a daunting experience, but I was determined to make the most of my second chance. I knew that I had to stay focused on my personal growth if I wanted to avoid falling back into old habits.

I remember feeling like I was in a constant battle with myself. The thoughts of using drugs were always there, lurking in the back of my mind, trying to find their way to the front. It was like a daunting memory that I had to consciously fight off every day. This war raged on for years, and I found myself in and out of prison, both federal and state.

But one day, something changed. I ended-up with a broken ankle from playing with my kids, and it turned into something much more serious. I developed sepsis, which sent me into septic shock. I died for 30 minutes, and when I came back, it was like a switch had been flipped inside me.

The experience was life-changing, but it didn't happen right away. It took time for me to fully process what had happened and to understand the gravity of the situation. I realized that I was tired of the person I saw in the mirror and that I needed to make a change.

It wasn't an easy road to recovery. I messed up a few times, but I learned that every mistake was an opportunity to learn and grow. It got easier to overcome my addiction over time, but it was never an easy walk.

I had to fight against my own thoughts and urges, and it felt like I was in a mini-war with myself. But I never gave up. I kept pushing forward, even when I felt like I was being dragged back down.

Looking back now, I'm proud of how far I've come. I've learned to be kinder to myself and to recognize that recovery is a journey, not a destination. It's a process that requires time, patience, and a lot of hard work.

If there's one thing, I want to leave you with, it's this: recovery is possible. No matter how difficult your journey may seem, there is always hope. You are capable of overcoming your addiction, and you deserve to live a happy, healthy life.

I started by finding a job and a place to live. I also started to take care of myself, both physically and mentally. I ate healthy foods, exercised regularly, and practiced meditation and mindfulness. I continued to read self-help books and attend counseling sessions.

But it wasn't just about me. I also wanted to give back to my community. I started volunteering at a local shelter for the homeless, and I used my experiences to inspire hope and deliver options for ways out to others who were struggling. I spoke at community centers, sharing my story and encouraging others to believe in themselves and their abilities.

As I continued to work on myself and give back to my community, I started to see the power of manifestation in action. I set goals for myself, both short-term and long-term, and I used visualization techniques to see myself achieving those goals. I used positive affirmations to remind myself that I was capable of success.

Today, I am proud of how far I have come. I have built a successful business, published a book, and inspired countless people to believe in themselves and their abilities. But I know that there is still more work to be done.

"Broken, But Not Destroyed"

The Healing Power of Writing Your Story "Kintsugi and the Redemption of Brokenness"

Chapter 3

When it comes to writing a note to yourself using the kintsugi method, you can apply a similar philosophy. Instead of trying to hide or ignore the brokenness or challenges in your life, you can use them as an opportunity to grow and transform into a stronger person.

To write a note to yourself using the kintsugi method, start by acknowledging the challenges or struggles you have faced. Then, reflect on what you have learned from these experiences and how they have shaped you into the person you are today. As you write, think about how you can use the lessons you have learned to move forward and create a new, beautiful story for yourself.

Just like the gold or silver used in kintsugi, you can use your experiences to add depth and richness to your story. By embracing and celebrating your imperfections, you can create a unique and beautiful work of art that tells the story of your life.

Here's MINE:

Dear Old Self,

I am writing this letter to say goodbye to you. I am saying goodbye to your old habits, your old lifestyle, and your drug addiction. I am also saying goodbye to the prison terms, both state and federal, that have kept you locked up for far too long.

It's time to leave all of that behind and start a new chapter in your life. I know it won't be easy, but trust me when I say that it will be worth it.

You have been through so much in your life, and it's time to use those experiences to your advantage. You are stronger than you think, and you have the power to overcome any obstacle that comes your way.

It's time to take control of your life and make the changes necessary to become the person you want to be. You have the ability to create a better future for yourself, and it all starts with leaving your old self behind.

You may feel scared or uncertain about what the future holds, but that's okay. Embrace the unknown and use it as an opportunity to grow and learn. Every step you take towards a better life will be worth it.

Remember, you are not defined by your past mistakes. You have the power to create a new identity for yourself and become the person you want to be. It's never too late to start fresh and create a better life for yourself.

Believe in yourself and your ability to succeed. Surround yourself with positive influences and people who will support you on your journey. You are not alone, and there are resources available to help you along the way.

I am proud of you for taking this step towards a better life. It takes courage to leave your old self behind and embrace the unknown. But I know you are capable of doing great things, and I can't wait to see what the future holds for you.

Goodbye, Old Self. It's time to start a new chapter in your life.

Sincerely,

Your Future Self

The letter I wrote is a powerful tool for anyone who is struggling with addiction, a criminal record, or other challenges in life that require them to make a significant change. It's a way of saying goodbye to the old self, the self that was defined by those challenges and struggles, and embracing a new, brighter future.

The letter is important because it provides a clear message of hope and encouragement to anyone who may be struggling with addiction or other challenges. It acknowledges the difficulties and struggles of the past, but it also emphasizes the importance of moving forward and making positive changes in one's life.

By saying goodbye to the old self, the letter encourages readers to let go of the past and start fresh. It emphasizes that individuals are not defined by their past mistakes, and that they have the power to create a new identity for themselves and become the person they want to be.

The letter also highlights the importance of taking control of one's life and making the changes necessary to create a better future. It acknowledges that this won't be easy and that there will be challenges along the way, but it encourages readers to embrace the unknown and use it as an opportunity to grow and learn.

The letter is also motivational in nature. It provides a message of hope and encouragement to readers, reminding them that they are not alone and that there are resources available to help them along the way. It encourages readers to believe in themselves and their ability to succeed, and to surround themselves with positive influences and people who will support them on their journey.

Overall, the letter is an important tool for anyone who is struggling with addiction, a criminal record, or other challenges in life. It provides a powerful message of hope and encouragement, and it emphasizes the importance of taking control of one's life and making positive changes for the future. For anyone who is looking to start fresh and create a better life for themselves, the letter provides a clear roadmap for doing that.

As someone who has experienced addiction, a criminal record, and other challenges in life, I know firsthand how difficult it can be to face these struggles. I understand what it's like to feel lost, alone, and uncertain about the future.

But I also know that it's possible to overcome these challenges and create a new, brighter future for yourself. That's why I wanted to write this letter to you, my audience. I wanted to share my story, my experiences, and my insights with others who may be struggling with similar challenges.

I wanted to provide a message of hope and encouragement to anyone who may be feeling lost or alone. I want to remind you that you are not defined by your past mistakes, and that you have the power to create a new future for yourself.

I also want to emphasize the importance of taking control of your life and making positive changes. I know that it's not easy, but I believe that it's worth it. I encourage you to take the first step towards a better life, because every step you take towards a better future will be worth it.

Ultimately, I wrote this letter to you because I believe that everyone deserves a second chance. I know that it's possible to overcome addiction, criminal records, and other challenges in life, and I want to share that message with you. I hope that my experiences can serve as a source of inspiration and motivation to you, and that you will use this letter as a tool to make positive changes in your life.

Remember, you are not alone, and there are resources available to help you on your journey. Believe in yourself and your ability to succeed, and know that you have the power to create a new future for yourself.

"Broken but not Destroyed"

Lost and Found. A Young Person's Journey Through Addiction and Betrayal"

CHAPTER 4

When I was 15 years old, I was pretty out of control. I would argue and fight with my siblings, and often run away for days at a time to do drugs and party. Looking back on it now, I realize that I was trying to escape from my problems rather than facing them head-on. I somehow managed to still go to school, but even then, I ended up dropping out and getting a GED.

If I could go back in time and talk to my 15-year-old self, I would tell myself to slow down and think things through before acting impulsively. I would tell myself that it's okay to make mistakes, but it's important to learn from them and grow as a person. I would also encourage myself to seek help and support from my family and friends, and to not be afraid to ask for help when I need it.

Unfortunately, things only got worse when my little brother and I got into an argument and my mom ended up calling the police on me. This wasn't the first time something like this had happened, and I was used to hearing the recommendation to "lock them up" from the police officers. As a result of my actions, I ended up in my first adult jail in Red Lake, Minnesota.

After my mom called the cops, I was taken to the Bay Pines juvenile facility. As a Native American boy, I was then transferred to the Red Lake Group Home in Red Lake, Minnesota. Unfortunately, my time there was not easy. I had trouble getting along with the other kids, and to make matters worse, a staff member, the secretary, continuously tried to sleep with me. She was 35 years old, and I was just a young teenager at the time.

Eventually, I got into a fight with two kids back-to-back, both of whom were my friends. I won those fights, but the group home had a zero-tolerance policy for violence, and as a result, they sent me to the Red Lake Minnesota jail.

Looking back on my life, it's hard to believe how far I've come. When I was 15 years old, I was a lost and troubled kid who was constantly getting into trouble. I was fighting with my siblings, running away from home, and getting into drugs and partying. I thought I knew everything and that I could handle life as an adult, but I was wrong.

My troubles only got worse when I ended up in jail at such a young age. The Red Lake jail was a disgusting place, and I still remember the scabies outbreak that affected everyone in there. I got into fights with older men, flooded my cell in frustration, and felt like my life was spiraling out of control.

Being in jail at such a young age was a surreal experience. It was overwhelming and scary, and I didn't know how to handle it. I felt like I was losing control of my life, and I didn't know what my future held.

During my time in jail, I acted out and got into trouble. I was angry and frustrated, and I didn't know how to deal with my emotions. Looking back on it now, I realize that I was just a scared and confused kid who was struggling to find his way in the world.

Eventually, I was released from jail, but my troubles didn't end there. I was put back in my mother's custody, but I didn't appreciate the opportunity I was given. Instead, I hung out with the wrong crowd and got into more trouble. I started to do more with drugs and alcohol, and it quickly spiraled out of control.

During those three months, I saw the ugliness of addiction firsthand. I saw how it can take over your life and turn you into someone you never thought you could be. I betrayed the trust of my family and friends, and I didn't care about the consequences of my actions.

I was lost and didn't know what to do with my life. I felt like I was in a never-ending cycle of pain and self-destruction. It wasn't until I hit rock bottom that I realized I needed help.

But even then, it wasn't easy. I had to confront the demons inside me and face the consequences of my actions. I had to make amends with the people I hurt and work hard to regain their trust.

Looking back, those three months were a dark time in my life. But I'm sharing this with you because I want you to know that it's okay to struggle. It's okay to make mistakes and fall down. What's important is that you get back up and keep fighting.

Keweenaw Academy

At the age of 16, I found myself in my second juvenile lock up detention center called the Keweenaw Academy. Looking back now, I realize that this facility was shut down completely three years later for the way that they were treating the kids. Unfortunately, I was one of the many kids who suffered abuse, both physically and emotionally, during my time there.

It's unfortunate that some people think that juvenile facilities are safe places where nothing bad happens. The reality is that many of these facilities have a history of abuse and neglect, and the kids who are sent there are often subjected to physical, emotional, and sometimes sexual abuse.

In my experience at the Keweenaw Academy, there were multiple staff members who were fired for having sexual relationships with the kids. The abuse wasn't just limited to sexual misconduct, though. The staff also used a restraint system that was incredibly violent and dangerous. I remember times when I was restrained by eight or more grown men, and they would punch and kick me while I was restrained.

Unfortunately, this kind of abuse is not uncommon in juvenile facilities. But there are ways to counteract it. First and foremost, we need to hold these facilities accountable for their actions. This means investigating reports of abuse thoroughly and punishing those who are responsible.

Another way to counteract the abuse in these facilities is to provide better training and support for the staff. Many of the staff members who work in these facilities are underpaid and overworked, and they may not have the resources they need to do their jobs effectively. By providing them with better training and support, we can help them to better understand how to work with troubled youth without resorting to violence or abuse.

Finally, we need to provide better alternatives to juvenile detention. Many of the kids who end up in these facilities are there because they come from difficult backgrounds or have experienced trauma. By providing them with better support and resources, we can help them to address the underlying issues that may be contributing to their behavior. This could include things like counseling, mentorship programs, and job training.

Overall, it's important that we take a hard look at the way we treat troubled youth in this country. By working to counteract the abuse that happens in juvenile facilities and providing better alternatives to detention, we can help to create a better future for these kids.

The reason I ended up in this facility was because My uncle Paul worked at the Keweenaw Academy, so he and my mom got together and came up with the idea to have me go there. They made a personal recommendation to the Judge and the judge said OK.

When I arrived, I quickly realized that I was one of only a few Native or Mexican kids there. The rest were black. The facility was like a boot camp. We had PT three times a day, and we were constantly working, doing things like shoveling snow, sometimes for up to 16 hours a day.

And if you got tired and stopped working, you were put into a full body restraint and 3 feet of snow every time you were at least punched once or twice knees on the head. It's a very traumatic experience. Especially, for young kids.

After my time at the Keweenaw Academy was up, I was released back to my mom, but nothing had really changed. I still found myself getting into trouble, and eventually, I became a criminal...

I learned the hard way that addiction and betrayal can destroy your life, but I also learned from my experiences, it's that it's never too late to change your life. No matter how lost or troubled you may feel, there is always hope for a better tomorrow.

"Broken but not Destroyed"
Standing Up for What's Right: The Fight with myself. Bark River Harris HS

CHAPTER 5

Bark river Harris years.

As I sit here and reflect on my past, I am filled with mixed emotions. It's been a long journey to get to where I am now, and I can't help but think about the choices I've made and the people who have influenced me along the way.

When I left the Keweenaw Academy, I was filled with a sense of relief. I had been counting down the days until I could leave that place and start fresh.

However, as I returned home, I couldn't help but feel resentful towards my mother. I blamed her for my choices and my actions. I felt like she had forced me to go to that place, and I was angry that I had to suffer the consequences of my mistakes.

I ended up enrolling in a small school called Bark River Harris School. It was a welcoming place, and I was glad to be there. My older brother had started attending that school in the 11th grade, and I followed suit when I got home. My brother and I were complete opposites. He always played by the rules and never got into trouble, whereas I was always getting into trouble.

On my very first day at Bark River Harris School, I got into a fight with a guy named Matt. Years later, Matt became a cop and a really good dude, but back then, I saw myself as a protector of the weak, and Matt was bullying a weaker student. I wasn't going to stand for that, so I stepped in and defended the weaker student. (Leroy)

As I think back to the fight with Matt, it's hard to believe that it was really just a quick exchange of punches. At the time, it felt like a much bigger deal, but looking back, it was really nothing more than a few swings and some dodging.

I remember walking out of the front doors of the school with Matt, feeling a sense of anticipation and nerves building up inside me. He was known as a boxer and had a reputation for bullying other kids, so I knew this was going to be a challenge.

As we squared off, Matt started jumping around like a boxer, swinging at me twice. I was able to slip both punches, and then I saw my opening. I hit him with a left, followed by a right, and he went down.

I couldn't believe it. Matt was bleeding everywhere, but he got back up and we exchanged the same combo again. This time, I was determined not to get my brother's clothes bloody, so I kept hitting him.

Thankfully, my friend Bubba was there to help me out, it's funny Bubba became a cop too He's a detective, and we quickly got into another friend's car and got out of there. The next day, we were both suspended from school.

Looking back on that moment now, I realize that I never really took the time to understand who Matt was or what he might have been going through. All I saw was a bully, and I wanted to stand up to him. But as my life went on and Matt became my daughter's uncle, I began to see glimpses of the man he really was.

It's funny how life works out sometimes. That fight with Matt may have been a small moment in my life, but it ended up connecting me to someone who would become an important part of my family. And it taught me an important lesson about looking beyond someone's reputation and trying to understand who they really are.

I realize now that it wasn't just about defending the weaker student. It was also about standing up for myself and proving that I wasn't going to be a pushover anymore. I had spent so much time feeling resentful towards my mother and blaming her for my choices, but in that moment, I realized that I had the power to make my own choices and to stand up for what I believed

After the fight with Matt, things started to settle down in my life. For the first time, I found myself hanging out with peers who didn't get into trouble. We were just normal kids, going to school and getting good grades. Football became my passion and purpose. Being a tackle was what I was good at, and it gave me a sense of belonging.

Despite finding a sense of normalcy, I still found myself getting into trouble. It was like I couldn't help it. But when I was 17, I met Tiffany. She was a really nice girl, and her parents were like angels. I was having troubles at home and was at odds with my mom, so I ended up getting kicked out. That's when Tiffany's parents took me in.

It was the first time in my life that I experienced a normal family dynamic. I tried my best to be what they wanted me to be, and things were good for a few years. But like everything else in my life, drugs started to mess things up again there's always a choice. What do you think?

When I was told that I couldn't play football anymore, everything started to go downhill. Football was my outlet and my purpose, and without it, I felt lost. I started to spiral out of control, and it seemed like everything I had worked for was slipping away.

Looking back on those years, it's hard to believe how much has changed. From the fight with Matt to living with Tiffany's family, my life has been a rollercoaster ride. But through it all, I've learned some important lessons about the value of family, the importance of finding your passion, and the dangers of drugs.

I may have made some mistakes along the way, but I've learned from them and grown as a person. And that's what life is all about - the ups and downs, the good and bad, the mistakes and the triumphs. It's what makes us who we are and helps us become the person we were meant to be.

My high school years and the people who were a part of it, it's hard not to feel a sense of regret and sadness. I remember the excitement of playing football, the rush of victory, and the camaraderie of the team. But all of that came crashing down when I was told I couldn't play anymore. The rules of the Michigan high school athlete's association had dictated my fate, and it felt like my whole world had crumbled around me.

I tried to salvage what I could of my senior year by focusing on my grades, but it was too little too late. I found myself slipping into a deep depression, feeling like I had lost everything that mattered to me. And then, in a moment of desperation, I made a terrible mistake. I stole less than $200, and it landed me in jail.

It's hard to describe the feeling of being in jail. The loss of freedom, the constant fear and anxiety, and the sense of shame and hopelessness that consumes you. But even as I sat there, I couldn't bring myself to care about anything anymore. My dreams of a better future, of going to college and pursuing my passions, all seemed like distant memories.

As the days turned into weeks, I began to realize that my life would never be the same again. The opportunities that I had taken for granted were now gone, and I was left with nothing but regret and uncertainty. I didn't know what the future held for me, or if I even had a future at all.

Thank you for listening to my story. I hope that it inspires you to stand up for what you believe in.

"Broken but not destroyed" struggling through the pain. But seeing the beauty.

CHAPTER 6

Growing up, I had a passion for football. It was my escape from the realities of my life. But when I was told I couldn't play, it felt like the rug had been pulled out from under me. I lost all hope and stopped believing in myself. I began to see my life as a series of disappointments and setbacks, and I believed that my circumstances were to blame.

This negative mindset consumed me for years, and I found myself on a path of self-destruction. I made poor choices and surrounded myself with people who only brought me down. I continued to make excuses for my failures and blamed others for my shortcomings. This had no benefit in the long run.

When I became a father at the age of 21, I thought that this would be the turning point in my life. I believed that my son would be the motivation I needed to make a change. But the reality was that I was running from the law for a home invasion. I justified my actions by telling myself that the man I was robbing was a drug dealer. But the truth was that he was the father of a friend, and I had betrayed his trust.

This realization hit me hard, and I felt a deep sense of shame and regret. I knew that I had to take responsibility for my life and the choices I had made. I made a commitment to change, but it was not easy.

I struggled to find a job and often found myself in trouble with the law. I battled addiction and had a difficult time staying sober. My life was a continuous cycle of ups and downs, and I felt like I was never going to break free from the cycle.

Despite my struggles, I never gave up on myself. I knew that I had to keep fighting for a better life, not just for myself but for my son. I continued to work on my sobriety and sought out counseling to help me deal with my past trauma.

As the years went on, I found myself stuck in a cycle of destructive behavior. I wanted a better life, but I didn't know how to make that happen. I continued down the same path, making the same mistakes, and hoping for a different outcome.

By the time I went to prison for the first time, I had six children, and I was only 27 years old. I entered the prison system feeling empty, like anything left of who I was. had been stolen by my addictive and destructive personality.

I was sent to prison for assault with the intent to cause great bodily harm less than murder. While the victim survived, it was a close call, and I could have been charged with murder. Looking back, I don't know if I would have handled the situation differently. At that time in my life, I was a very violent person, and the injustice committed against my family member was horrendous. In that moment, I felt like I had to protect my little sister, and I acted out of anger.

But the consequences of my actions were severe. Since the Bureau of Indian Affairs has jurisdiction when a tribal member commits a felony, why? I was automatically sentenced to federal prison time. I just didn't realize what was in store for me.

I was sent to Hazelton USP, which was one of the toughest federal prisons in the country. It was a violent and dangerous place, and I felt like I was constantly looking over my shoulder. I was surrounded by hardened criminals, and I felt like I had no hope for a better future.

Let me tell you, being incarcerated at Hazleton United States Penitentiary was one of the toughest experiences of my life. I made some mistakes early on, trying to navigate the complex and dangerous world of prison politics. The reality is, prison is a microcosm of the outside world, with its own set of rules and power structures. And in federal prison, especially in the United States Penitentiaries, those power structures are controlled by gangs.

Make no mistake, these gangs have tentacles that reach into every aspect of prison life. They control the drug trade, the black market, and even the staff. Yes, you heard that right, the staff. It may be hard to believe, but the truth is that the gangs have infiltrated the prison staff and their families. So, the idea that the staff run any of these penitentiaries is nonsense.

The harsh reality is that all prisons are run by the gang members. They decide who gets what, who lives and who dies. And they do not hesitate to use violence to maintain their power. I was part of a group myself, and I can tell you that we were vicious. We did what we had to do to survive, and sometimes that meant hurting others.

I wish I could tell you that there is an easy solution to surviving in prison, but the truth is that there isn't. The best advice I can give you is to stay out of trouble, keep your head down, and try to stay out of the gangs' way. But even then, there are no guarantees.

Prison is a harsh and unforgiving place. It is a place where the strong prey on the weak, and the rules are made by those with the most power. And unfortunately, there are no easy solutions to surviving in such an environment. All we can do is hope to make it out alive and try to rebuild our lives once we are free.

There are a lot of things that I regret. I made some mistakes that I am not proud of, and I choose not to talk about them because I do not want to promote the violent aspects of prison life. Yes, it was a very real reality, but it is not something that I want to glorify.

But despite all of this, I knew that I had to try to make something of myself. I enrolled in educational programs and tried to stay out of trouble. I made friends with some of the other inmates and found support in unexpected places.

It wasn't easy, and there were days when I felt like giving up. But I knew that I had to keep pushing forward, not just for myself but for my children. I wanted to show them that even when things seem impossible, there is always hope for a better future.

This Year, my oldest son is graduating high school, and I couldn't be prouder of him. He's accomplished so much despite the challenges he's faced as the child of a father in prison. It's not the life I would have chosen for him, but I'm grateful that he's made the best of it.

My journey has been one of pain, struggle, and regret. But it's also been one of growth, learning, and redemption. I've learned that even in the darkest moments, there is always a glimmer of hope. And I've learned that it's never too late to turn your life around, no matter how dire the circumstances may seem.

When I was released from Hazleton United States Penitentiary in March 2015, I had a bright outlook on my future. I was determined to turn my life around and make something of myself. I transitioned out of prison using the halfway house and stayed there for six months, building a routine and trying to get my life back on track.

I decided to take up mixed martial arts as a way of channeling my anger and building up my self-confidence. I thought that if I could excel in the cage, I could prove to myself and others that I was a changed person. But things did not go as planned.

I had my first fight, and I was beaten. I ended up in the hospital, and they gave me painkillers to manage the pain. It wasn't long before I became addicted to them again. I fell back into old habits, and my life began to spiral out of control once again.

I wish I had made different choices. I wish I had found healthier ways of channeling my anger and dealing with my addiction. But at the time, I was lost and struggling to find my place in the world.

My journey after prison has been filled with ups and downs. While I am grateful for my release and the chance to start over, I know that there are no easy solutions to the challenges that come with rebuilding your life after incarceration. It takes hard work, dedication, and a willingness to seek help when you need it.

"Broken but not Destroyed "the realization!!

CHAPTER 7

I realize that it was the difficult times that made me who I am today. It took me three prison terms to finally understand that the source of my problems was myself. But once I had a clear path in mind, I started looking for solutions in the right places.

My life has been a rollercoaster of chaos and destruction. Looking back, I can see how reckless and irresponsible I was, putting myself and others in danger without a second thought. I was always chasing after the next thrill, the next high, without any regard for the consequences.

One of my secrets! was going out to the bars and watching people. I would wait for the big spenders, the guys who would flaunt their money and try to impress the ladies. I knew that these guys were easy targets, and I would wait patiently for my chance to strike.

When the bars closed and the lights came on, I would prowl the streets, looking for my next victim. I would follow them, waiting for the right moment to make my move. Sometimes it was a quick grab-and-run, other times I would use a distraction or a fake-out to get what I wanted. It wasn't pretty, but it was effective.

I knew that what I was doing was wrong, but I couldn't stop myself. I was addicted to the rush of adrenaline that came with each successful heist. I felt invincible, like nothing could touch me.

But my reckless behavior caught up with me in the end. I was arrested for possession of analogue and sentenced to time in the Michigan Department of Corrections. It was a wake-up call for me, a sign that I needed to turn my life around.

I spent a considerable amount of time in the Michigan Department of Corrections, where I met a lot of people. But there was only one person who really became like family to me - my brother Chris. By the time I entered the prison system, I had already served time twice before, so I knew the importance of staying out of trouble and focusing on self-improvement. This mindset proved to be crucial during my time in the Michigan State Prison, which was an entirely different beast.

Chris and I met at a prison in Munising, Michigan, which was classified as a level two facility. However, there was always the potential for violence. Thankfully, the unit where we were housed was relatively laid-back, which allowed us to focus on our personal goals. During our time together, we formulated a plan for success that we both continue to execute to this day.

I'm proud to say that Chris and I remain friends to this day. However, I must admit that my time in the prison system was incredibly traumatic. The Michigan Department of Corrections can be an incredibly challenging and unpredictable environment.

Many inmates face violence, abuse, and other forms of mistreatment while incarcerated. It's essential that we work towards creating a more just and equitable criminal justice system that prioritizes rehabilitation and support for those who have been impacted by the system.

Prison was a difficult and humbling experience. It gave me time to reflect on my past mistakes and think about what I wanted for my future. I knew that I couldn't keep living the way I had been, always on the lookout for my next score. I needed to find a new path, something that would give me purpose.

I can see how destructive my behavior was. I put myself and others in danger, and caused untold harm to innocent people. But I am determined to use my experiences to help others, to show them that there is a way out of the darkness and into the light.

I knew I needed to change my environment, so I relocated to Iron Mountain, Michigan. When I was released, that's where I found a job welding snowplows, and for the first time in my life, I was happy without drugs. It wasn't an easy road, but I stayed consistent on the plan I created and kept pushing forward.

Every day, I woke up at 5 am, hit the gym, and then went to work. It was a routine that kept me grounded and helped me stay focused on my goals. I started making friends at work and got involved in the community.

There were times when I wanted to give up and go back to my old ways, but I knew that wasn't the life I wanted anymore. I wanted to be a better person, contribute to society, and make a difference. So, I stuck with it and kept pushing forward.

Life is full of challenges, but I've learned that it's how we respond to those challenges that defines us. I'm grateful for the second chance I was given, and I'm not going to waste it. I'm going to keep pushing forward, and I'm excited to see where this journey takes me next.

But even though everything was looking up, I still couldn't help, but remember when that muzzle was shoved into my face, I can still hear the boom from the pistol. I can still feel the throbbing pain in my arm where the bullet had entered me. It was a sensation that no number of drugs could have prepared me for. My mind was racing, trying to make sense of what had just happened, but everything seemed to be a blur. The sound of the gunshot still echoed in my ears, drowning out all other noise.

I remembered putting my arm in front of my face, as if trying to shield myself from what was coming. It was a reflex action, one that I had no control over. But somehow, it had saved my life. The bullet had gone in by my elbow, leaving a deep gash on my arm.

I tried to get up, but my body wouldn't cooperate. The pain was intense, and my head was spinning. I looked around, trying to make sense of my surroundings. It was a dark blur, and I could see no one around clearly. The only thing that greeted me was the sound of my own labored breathing.

As I lay there, bleeding, I couldn't help but think about how I had ended up in this situation. It all started when I convinced my friends to take a ride to Green Bay, a place that I had once called home. I wanted to relive the memories, to feel the rush of excitement that came with being in a place that was once familiar.

But as soon as we got to the biker bar, things started to go wrong. I could sense the tension in the air, the hostility that seemed to emanate from every corner. It was as if everyone was out to get me, and I had no idea why.

And then, the gunshot.

I felt a deep sense of betrayal as I realized that my friends had abandoned me in my time of need.

They were nowhere to be found, leaving me alone in a sea of possible enemies. It was a stark reminder of how alone I truly was, how my addiction had driven away the people who once cared about me.

As the pain in my arm intensified, I knew that I needed to get help. I dragged myself to the back of the bar where I parked, hoping that my friends would hear my cries for help. It felt like an eternity before I finally saw the flashing lights of an ambulance in the distance.

The next few days were a blur of hospital being in intensive care unit. I knew that I had narrowly escaped death, and that it was time for me to make a change. I couldn't continue down this path of self-destruction, not if I wanted to live.

Looking back on that night, I realized that it was a wake-up call. It was a reminder that life is precious, and that we should never take it for granted. It was time for me to leave behind my old life, and start anew.

"Broken but not Destroyed" Meet Mom and Dad! And my Influences.

CHAPTER 8

Growing up, my mother was always an inspiration to me. Despite all the obstacles she faced as a single mother of five children, she never lost her strength and determination. She taught me the importance of good values and always tried her best to provide for our family, even if it meant working two jobs.

As the second oldest child, I often felt helpless as I watched my mother struggle to make ends meet. Looking back, I realize now just how much stress she was under and how little I did to help. But my mother never gave up. She continued to be the best version of herself every day, and I couldn't be prouder of her.

Unfortunately, my father's influence often overruled my mother's. I longed for a father figure in my life, but my mother knew that he was bad for me. She fought tooth and nail every second of the way to protect me from his negative influence.

Despite all the challenges she faced, my mother never gave up on her quest to break the generational curse that had haunted our family for so long. She believed in the power of choice, and she taught me that how we react to the choices we are faced with can make all the difference.

Looking back on my childhood, I realize now just how hard my mother worked to give us a better life. She sacrificed so much for our sake, and I am forever grateful for everything she has done for me.

Today, my mother continues to inspire me with her strength and resilience. She is the embodiment of the phrase "never give up," and I am honored to call her my mom. I love you, Mom, and I will always be grateful for everything you have done for me.

My father and I had a complicated relationship. When he was released from prison, I was still young and didn't fully understand the dynamics of a father-son relationship. Despite this, my dad quickly became my best friend, while also being very strict with me. I craved a more traditional father-son relationship with him, but I think he did what he thought was necessary as a man raising a child. Looking back, I realize that my dad didn't fully understand the concept of breaking generational curses, but he did set up the building blocks for me to succeed.

However, our relationship wasn't without its challenges. My dad used to beat me and was very militant towards me. Despite this, I knew deep down that he was a loving dad who wanted the best for me. As I grew older, I began to see a softer side of my dad. He became kinder and more loving towards me, and I could tell that he was proud of the person I was becoming.

Sadly, my dad passed away on August 3, 2012. I received the news while I was in prison, and it hit me hard. I missed him terribly and wished that I could have had more time with him. Despite the challenges we faced, I know that my dad loved me and that he did the best he could with the tools he had.

In many ways, my dad's passing made me realize that life is precious, and that we should cherish the time we have with our loved ones. It also motivated me to become a better person and break the cycle of generational curses that had plagued my family for generations.

Today, I'm proud of the person I've become. I've worked hard to overcome the challenges I faced growing up, and I know that my dad would be proud of me too. While I still miss him dearly, I take comfort in knowing that his love and guidance helped shape me into the person I am today.

My grandpa Pete was one of the most influential figures in my life. He was a good man through and through, and I learned so much from him. He was a hard man, old-school and didn't put up with any nonsense. He would always tell it like it is, and I loved that about him. I inherited so many of his characteristics, and I am proud to carry them with me every day.

My grandpa was a true inspiration to me. He taught me how to build a deck, how to build a house, and how to work on cars. He was always there to lend a helping hand, and he never hesitated to teach me something new.

Sadly, my grandpa passed away from what they said was Covid, but in reality, it was lung cancer. It's frustrating how hospitals can tell you lies sometimes. I remember the day I found out he had passed away. It was a shock to me, and I was devastated. It was as if a part of me had died with him.

But looking back, I realize that my grandpa had been preparing me for his departure all along. He never told me he loved me until I was 21 years old. I think it was because he was going in for a quadruple bypass surgery, but he made sure to never keep it a secret from me after that.

My grandpa loved me, and he showed me in so many ways before he died. I miss him every day, but I know that he is with me in spirit. He lives on through me, and I am proud to carry on his legacy.

grandpa Pete was a major influence on my life. He taught me the value of hard work, perseverance, and to never give up. I will always cherish the memories I have of him, and I am forever grateful for everything he did for me. I love you, grandpa, and I know that you are watching over me from heaven.

It's difficult to find the right words to express the depth of my emotions when I think about my auntie Jean and my uncle Mike. They were such an important part of my life, and losing them both was a devastating blow. I remember how excited I was to see them when I was released from prison, but the news my uncle's passing shattered me. And then my auntie died the same week as my grandpa Pete these were definitely devastating blows.

My uncle Mike was always the life of the party, and he had a way of making everyone feel welcome. He took me fishing and hunting, and those memories will always be cherished. Even when I was at my lowest, he never gave up on me. I know he was hurting inside, watching me struggle with addiction, but he never stopped loving me.

My auntie Jean was a force to be reckoned with. She was tough as nails, but if you were lucky enough to be loved by her, you knew you had someone in your corner for life. She was there for me from the very beginning, delivering me into this world and always looking out for me. I remember how she would make moccasins for me, always wanting to make sure I had something special. When I think about her, I can still hear her laughter.

But I know that I caused them both a great deal of pain. They had to watch me spiral out of control, and I know that hurt them deeply. I regret that I didn't get the chance to talk to my auntie Jean before she passed. I wish I could tell her how much she meant to me, and how sorry I am for the pain I caused.

Even though my auntie Jean and my uncle Mike are no longer with us, they continue to be major influences in my life. The lessons they taught me, the love they gave me, and the memories we shared continue to guide me to this day.

My uncle Mike showed me what it means to be a true friend. He was always there for me, no matter what. Even when I was in prison, he would write me letters and send me care packages. He never judged me for my mistakes, and he always believed in me. He showed me how to be kind, compassionate, and understanding. He taught me how to fish and hunt, and those skills have stayed with me over the years. Whenever I'm out in nature, I feel his presence with me.

My auntie Jean was a tough love kind of person. She didn't mince words, and she didn't suffer fools gladly. But underneath her tough exterior was a heart of gold. She loved fiercely and protected those she cared about. She showed me what it means to be loyal and devoted. She made moccasins for me and cooked me meals. She was like a second

mother to me. Even though she could be tough at times, I knew that she loved me with all her heart.

My grandpa Pete was a quiet man, but he had a strong presence. He taught me the value of hard work and perseverance. He worked tirelessly to provide for his family. He was a man of few words, but his actions spoke volumes.

All of these people continue to be major influences in my life. Whenever I'm faced with a difficult decision, I think about what my uncle Mike would do. Whenever I'm feeling lost, I think about my auntie Jean and how she would guide me. Whenever I'm working hard, I think about my grandpa Pete and how he never gave up. They are a part of me, and their memories give me strength and courage.

I miss them all so much, and I wish they were still here with me. But I know that they're watching over me from above. Their love and guidance continue to shape my life, and I'm grateful for every moment I had with them. Even though they're gone, their legacies live on. They will always be a part of me, and I will always be grateful for the impact they had on my life.

"Broken but not Destroyed" We're all faced with choices. What path will you choose?

CHAPTER 9

I made some choices that led me down a dark path. I was drawn to the excitement and freedom that came with making bad decisions, but I soon realized that the consequences were severe. This path was a trap, designed to imprison me in a cycle of negativity and self-destructive behavior.

One of the biggest dangers of the bad path was drug use. In the United States, drug use among juveniles is a serious problem. According to the National Institute on Drug Abuse (NIDA), nearly 10% of 8th graders, 23% of 10th graders, and 36% of 12th graders reported using illicit drugs in the past year. This includes marijuana, prescription drugs, and other illegal substances.

Drug use can have devastating effects on the developing brain. Studies have shown that drug use during adolescence can lead to long-term changes in brain function and structure. It can impair memory, attention, and learning, and can increase the risk of mental health disorders.

In addition to the physical and mental health risks, drug use can also have legal consequences. Juveniles who are caught using or possessing illegal drugs can face charges and legal penalties that can impact their future opportunities.

The bad path wasn't just about drug use, though. It was a cycle of negative behaviors that led to even more negative consequences. It was a path of self-destruction that robbed me of my potential and left me with deep scars.

Despite the challenges, I learned an important lesson: it's never too late to make positive changes in your life. I sought help and support from various resources, such as therapy, support through a program, I created call resilience. Over time, I began to understand that the bad path wasn't worth it. The excitement and freedom that I had been seeking were all temporary, and the consequences were severe.

I recall a time when I was in high school, and it was undoubtedly one of the toughest times in my life. I was lost, and I didn't know who I was or where I belonged. It was such a weird and confusing time for me. I wanted to fit in with a crowd and be accepted, so I ended up fitting in with everybody. However, fitting in with everybody wasn't a good thing because I was drawn to acceptance.

During my younger years, I was always trying to impress somebody, be it my peers or adults. The truth is that I was living in fear, and I was afraid of what others would think of me. I was afraid of being rejected or not being liked anymore. I never understood what it meant to be important to myself and only care about what I thought about myself. I didn't realize that being comfortable with the decisions I made was more important than being accepted by others.

It pains me to think about the problems that some kids face during their teenage years. Statistics reveal that teen suicides, teen rapes, and teen pregnancies occur frequently among both boys and girls. These problems are severe and can lead to devastating consequences for those involved.

Teen suicide is a prevalent problem, with suicide being the second leading cause of death among teenagers. The statistics are alarming, and it's heartbreaking to think about how many young lives are lost every year. It's crucial for us to recognize the signs of depression and offer support to those who are struggling.

Teen rape is another significant issue, with one in six women and one in thirty-three men experiencing sexual assault before the age of 18. It's essential to educate young people about consent and healthy relationships to prevent such incidents from occurring.

Teen pregnancy is also a concerning issue, with the United States having one of the highest rates of teen pregnancy among developed countries. It's crucial for young people to have access to comprehensive sex education and contraception to prevent unintended pregnancies.

We can raise awareness about the problems that teenagers face and work together to create a safer and more supportive world for young people.

I realize that mentioning my teen years is crucial when talking about my path. It's evident from my autobiography that I had strayed from the path I should have taken. I could have rectified my path at any time, but the deeper I got, the more I said, "fuck it" to committing petty or even violent crimes. At that time, my life amounted to nothing, and the crazy thing is, I wore it like a badge of honor. Looking back now, I still can't make sense of how I was okay with victimizing so many people.

During those teen years, I was lost and confused. I didn't know who I was or where I belonged. I was always trying to impress somebody, be it my peers or adults. I was living in fear, and I was afraid of what others would think of me. I was afraid of being rejected or not being liked anymore. I never understood what it meant to be important to myself and only care about what I thought about myself. I didn't realize that being comfortable with the decisions I made was more important than being accepted by others.

I was drawn to acceptance, and I wanted to fit in with a crowd, so I ended up fitting in with everybody. However, fitting in with everybody wasn't a good thing because it only led me down a path of self-destruction. I was committing crimes and hurting people, and it was all because I was trying to find a sense of belonging.

Looking back on those years, I realize how lucky I am to be alive. I could have easily been killed or ended up in jail for the rest of my life. But I believe that there is a God, and He had His hands on me at all times. If not for His intervention, I would not be here today.

Now, I've turned my life around, and I'm committed to making a positive impact on the world. I'm not defined by my past, and I've learned from my mistakes. I'm grateful for the second chance that I've been given, and I'm determined to make the most of it.

It's essential for young people to understand the importance of making good decisions and being comfortable with who they are. It's crucial to recognize the signs of depression and offer support to those who are struggling. Teen suicide, teen rape, and teen pregnancy are prevalent problems that we need to address as a society. We need to educate young people about consent, healthy relationships.

My story is a reminder that it's never too late to turn your life around. No matter how lost you may feel, there is always a way back to the right path. It takes courage, determination, and a willingness to change, but it's worth it. I hope that by sharing my story, I can inspire others to make positive changes in their lives and make a difference in the world.

"Broken but not Destroyed"
Uncle no name...

CHAPTER 10

Uncle NO Name:

When I first arrived in Tennessee, I was a young and wild person, eager to experience life to the fullest. I rented a trailer right next to my uncle's house, who happened to be a bit of a troublemaker himself. He taught me all sorts of things about how to live on the edge and be a criminal. Looking back, I realize now how misguided and foolish I was, but at the time, I thought I was invincible.

One night, my uncle and I were sitting around when our friend Raymond came up in conversation. Raymond was a guy we both knew who sold weed and had a reputation for growing some of the best around.

He had six enormous marijuana plants growing in his backyard, each one standing at least six feet tall. My uncle and I decided that we wanted to get our hands on those plants, but there was one major obstacle in our way: Raymond's two big, aggressive pit bulls.

We didn't let the dogs deter us, though. Instead, we came up with a plan to distract them. I suggested that we start feeding them treats so that they would be less likely to attack us when we snuck into the backyard. So, one night, we crept along the fence that separated Raymond's yard from my uncle's, which was only about a foot high. We made our way to the back of the yard, where we tossed some treats over the fence and into the pit bulls' territory. The dogs devoured the treats eagerly, wagging their tails as they chomped away.

With the dogs pacified, my uncle and I climbed over the fence and made our way to the marijuana plants. We quickly cut them down and hauled them back to our trailer, feeling like we had pulled off a major heist.

remembering another wild and crazy night when I was living in Tennessee. I was a 17-year-old kid with no rules and no sense of responsibility, and my uncle was only too happy to teach me all the tricks of the criminal trade. This particular night, we were out driving around town, looking for trouble, when we saw a car that caught our attention.

The car was a flashy sports car, and my uncle recognized it as belonging to a local drug dealer. He turned to me and said, "Let's go get that car."

I was a bit hesitant at first, but my uncle was persuasive, and before I knew it, we were tailing the drug dealer's car through the streets of Tennessee. We followed him to a seedy part of town, where he parked the car and went into a rundown apartment building. My uncle and I parked a few blocks away and waited.

After a few minutes, the drug dealer came back out of the building and got into his car. My uncle and I waited until he started driving away, and then we followed him again. This time, we were much closer to his car, and my uncle was driving like a madman, swerving in and out of traffic to keep up.

Finally, the drug dealer pulled into a parking lot and got out of his car. My uncle parked our car a few spaces away, and he got out and approached him. My uncle was demanding that he hand over the drugs

To my surprise, the drug dealer didn't put up a fight. He handed over the dope and my uncle drove off with his new sports car, leaving the drug dealer standing in the parking lot, stunned and helpless.

As we drove away, I couldn't believe what we had just done. But my uncle was ecstatic, laughing and whooping as he drove through the streets of Tennessee in his new ride. For a while, I felt like I was on top of the world, living life on the edge and feeling invincible.

But things would always have to end up in a bar. But at least I can tell you about the first black girl I ever kissed she had a gold tooth her name is Jazmine. My uncle and I decided to hit up a local nightclub in Tennessee called Denim and Diamonds. It was a popular spot for locals and tourists alike, with a rowdy crowd and loud music that could be heard from blocks away.

We arrived at the club just after midnight, and I could already feel the energy in the air. My uncle was dressed to impress, wearing a flashy suit and a wide-brimmed hat, while I was more casual in jeans and a t-shirt. We paid the cover charge and made our way inside, mind you I'm only 17 years old, but we made our way to where the bass was thumping and the dance floor was packed.

As we made our way through the crowd, I spotted a beautiful black girl across the room. She was dancing with a group of her friends, and I couldn't take my eyes off her. My uncle noticed my gaze and elbowed me, saying, "Go talk to her, kid. What are you waiting for?"

I hesitated at first, but my uncle wasn't one to take no for an answer. He pushed me towards the girl and said, "Introduce yourself. You never know where it might lead."

So, with a deep breath, I made my way over to the girl and introduced myself. Her name was Jasmine, and she was even more beautiful up close. We hit it off right away, talking and laughing as if we had known each other for years.

As the night wore on, we danced together and drank a few shots of tequila. My uncle was nowhere to be found, but I didn't care. I was having the time of my life with Jasmine, and nothing else mattered.

At one point, we stepped out onto the balcony for some fresh air, and Jasmine pulled me into a passionate kiss. It was my first kiss with a black girl, and I felt like I was on top of the world. We spent the rest of the night together, dancing and laughing and enjoying each other's company.

The next morning, I woke up with a pounding headache and a vague sense of honor. I was just young. My uncle was already up and dressed, looking at me with a knowing grin. He said, "Looks like you had a good time last night, kid. Maybe next time you'll remember to pace yourself."

I smiled weakly and nodded, feeling both embarrassed and exhilarated by the experience. I knew that I had a lot to learn about life and love, but for that one wild and crazy night in Denim and Diamonds, I felt like anything was possible.

But eventually, we left Tennessee on the dream, of running a business in Florida. As I sat in the passenger seat of my uncle's beat-up old pickup truck, I couldn't help but feel a sense of excitement and anticipation. We were on our way back to Florida, where I would be joining my uncle in running his Eagles cuts his company. It was a door-to-door steak selling business, and it had been a Way out for him.

I had always looked up to my uncle Jamie, who was a male role model to me. He was a charismatic and charming man, with a devil-may-care attitude that I found thrilling. He had always been there for me, ever since I was a little boy, and I felt like I owed him everything.

But as we drove through the hot, humid Florida countryside, I began to notice things about my uncle that I had never noticed before. He was always on the phone, talking in hushed tones to people I didn't know. He would disappear for hours at a time, leaving me alone in the truck with nothing to do but stare out at the passing scenery.

As we started to meet with the other members of the Eagles cuts team, I began to see a darker side of my uncle's business dealings. He would make promises to customers that he knew he couldn't keep, and he would pressure his employees to sell more and more, even if it meant lying to customers or taking advantage of them.

I tried to ignore these things at first, telling myself that it was just the way things were done in the business world. But as time went on, I began to realize that my uncle was not the man I had always thought he was. He was manipulative, selfish, and ruthless in his pursuit of success.

And as I spent more time with him, I began to feel the same darkness creeping into my own soul. I became short-tempered and violent, taking risks that I knew were foolish and dangerous. I started to feel like I was addicted to the adrenaline rush of our lifestyle, always chasing after the next big score.

But despite all of this, I couldn't bring myself to leave my uncle or the Eagles cuts business. It was all I had ever known, and I felt like I owed it to my uncle to carry on the tradition now I know he just manipulated me to feel bad. So, I stayed, even though I knew that it was slowly destroying me.

I realize how foolish I was to think that this was the life to live. It was an endless pit of never being satisfied, always searching for something more. And it wasn't until I finally broke free from my uncle's influence that I was able to see just how much damage he had done to me.

But even though it was a painful and difficult experience, I wouldn't trade it for anything. It taught me the valuable lesson that sometimes the people we look up to the most are not always the heroes we thought they were. And it showed me that sometimes the only way to find true happiness and fulfillment is to walk away from the things that are holding us back.

Looking back now, I realize how foolish and dangerous our actions were. We could have been caught, or worse, someone could have been hurt or killed. But at the time, I was young and reckless, and my uncle was a bad influence on me. It took me a long time to realize that the criminal lifestyle was not the way to go. I was lucky to get out of it relatively unscathed, but not everyone is so fortunate. These days, I try to live a more honest and responsible life, and I hope that my experiences can serve as a warning to others who might be tempted to go down the same path I did.

"Broken but not Destroyed" Meet Jack.

CHAPTER 11

As a warning to anyone reading this, the following story contains graphic and potentially triggering content related to drug abuse. Names situations and scenarios have been altered to protect the people involved

Once upon a time, there was a young man named Jack. He was a football player in high school and had dreams of playing in college. However, one night after a game, Jack was involved in a car accident that left him with a severe injury to his leg. He was rushed to the hospital and had to undergo surgery to repair the damage.

In the aftermath of the accident, Jack was prescribed powerful painkillers to manage his pain. At first, he took them as directed by his doctor, but as time went on and his pain persisted, he found himself taking more and more of the pills to achieve the same level of relief.

Before he knew it, Jack had developed a full-blown addiction to the painkillers. He would do anything to get his hands on more of them, even resorting to buying them illegally on the street. His addiction took a toll on his relationships with his family and friends, and he began to isolate himself from everyone except for his dealer.

One day, Jack's dealer offered him something new - a drug called bath salts. He had heard of them before, but had never tried them. The dealer assured Jack that they would give him an even stronger high than the painkillers he was used to.

As soon as Jack took the bath salts, he knew he had made a terrible mistake. The high was intense and overwhelming, and he soon found himself hallucinating and experiencing terrifying delusions. He felt like he was being chased by monsters and that his skin was crawling with insects.

Despite the horror of the experience, Jack couldn't stop taking the bath salts. He was addicted to the rush they gave him, even though he knew they were destroying his mind and body.

One night, Jack took a particularly large dose of bath salts. He was alone in his apartment, and as the drug took hold of him, he began to feel like he was losing his mind. He saw demons crawling out of the walls and heard voices whispering in his ear. He tried to fight back against the hallucinations, but they only grew stronger and more terrifying.

As the night wore on, Jack's heart began to race and his breathing became shallow. He was sweating profusely and felt like he was on fire. He knew something was seriously wrong, but he was too high to call for help.

Eventually, Jack's heart gave out and he collapsed on the floor. By the time the paramedics arrived, it was too late to save him. He was pronounced dead at the scene, a victim of his own addiction to bath salts.

Losing a friend is never easy. It's something that shakes you to your core and leaves you feeling lost and alone. That's exactly how I felt when I found out that Jack had passed away.

Jack was one of my closest friends in high school. We bonded over a shared love of football and spent countless hours practicing and playing together. When he was injured in the car accident, I was right there by his side, offering support and encouragement as he went through his recovery.

But as time went on, things started to change. Jack became more distant and irritable, and he stopped coming to practice and games. I didn't know what was going on with him, but I could tell that something was seriously wrong.

It wasn't until later that I found out about Jack's addiction to painkillers. I was stunned and heartbroken to learn that my friend was struggling with something so serious and dangerous. I wanted to help him, but I didn't know how.

The news of Jack's death hit me like a ton of bricks. I couldn't believe that he was gone, that I would never see him again or hear his laugh or share a game with him. It was like a part of me had been ripped away, and I didn't know how to cope with the pain.

Dealing with Jack's family and loved ones was one of the hardest things I've ever had to do. They were all so devastated and in shock, and I felt like I was intruding on their grief. But I knew that I needed to be there for them, to offer support and a shoulder to cry on.

As we mourned Jack's passing, we talked a lot about the dangers of drug addiction. We all knew that drugs were bad, but none of us had ever thought it would happen to someone we knew and loved. It was a wake-up call for all of us, a reminder that even something as innocuous as a prescription from a doctor can lead down a dark and dangerous road.

I think what hit me the hardest was realizing that I could have done more to help Jack. Maybe if I had noticed the signs of his addiction earlier, or if I had reached out to him more often, things could have turned out differently. But I know that dwelling on the past won't bring him back, and that the best thing I can do now is to honor his memory and spread awareness about the dangers of drug addiction.

Jack's story is a tragic example of just how dangerous drug addiction can be. It's easy to think that drugs are something that only happens to "other people," but the reality is that anyone can fall victim to addiction.

One of the biggest dangers of drug use is the way it can take over your life. Jack started out taking prescription painkillers to manage his injury, but before he knew it, he was completely dependent on them. He would do anything to get more of the pills, even if it meant putting himself in danger or breaking the law.

This kind of addiction can have devastating consequences on your health. As Jack discovered when he started using bath salts, drugs can cause serious damage to your body and mind. The hallucinations and delusions he experienced were not only terrifying, but they were also a sign that his brain was being irreparably damaged by the drugs.

Drug addiction can also take a toll on your relationships with your family and friends. Jack became increasingly isolated and withdrawn as his addiction took hold, which only made things worse for him in the long run. When he passed away, his family and loved ones were left to pick up the pieces and try to make sense of what had happened.

Another danger of drug use is that it can be incredibly difficult to break the cycle of addiction. Even when you know that the drugs are causing you harm, the addiction can be so strong that it's hard to stop using them. This can lead to a vicious cycle of dependency and withdrawal, which can be incredibly hard to break without professional help.

Finally, it's important to remember that drugs can be deadly. Jack's story is a tragic reminder that even something as seemingly harmless as bath salts can have fatal consequences. When you're using drugs, you're putting your life on the line, and there's no guarantee that you'll survive the experience.

Overall, Jack's story is a powerful reminder that drug addiction is a serious and dangerous issue that affects millions of people around the world. If you or someone you know is struggling with addiction, it's important to seek help as soon as possible. With the right support and treatment, it's possible to break the cycle of addiction and start on the road to recovery.

The tragic story of Jack serves as a cautionary tale about the dangers of drug addiction. No matter how desperate you may feel, it's never worth risking your life for a temporary high. If you or someone you know is struggling with addiction, it's important to seek help before it's too late.

Even as I write this, it's a reminder to me of how very close I came many of times ending up like Jack in my addiction. I think God that he released me from them chains.

"Broken but not Destroyed"
Rambling man bad decisions...

CHAPTER 12

I always had an insatiable desire to explore the world around me. I found myself drawn to the unknown, to the uncharted territories. I always had a sense of wanderlust. The world seemed so vast and full of possibilities, and I longed to explore every inch of it. So, as soon as I was old enough to drive, I set out on a journey that would take me to the farthest reaches of the United States. Florida...

I remember the day like it was yesterday. I had just dropped out of high school, which was not the best decision and I did get a GED, but I was itching to hit the open road. I didn't want to wait and I didn't have a plan, or a destination in mind, but I knew that I had to keep moving until I found what I was looking for.

I got into my 1992 Grand Am and started driving. I watched as the world passed me by, the wind in my hair and the thrill of the open road stretching out before me. I drove for hours and hours, losing myself in the beauty of the world around me.

It was during this journey I found myself in Florida, a place that would forever change my life. I was struck by the beauty of the state, the palm trees swaying in the breeze and the scent of the ocean filling my nostrils.

I didn't have much money to my name, just $50 in my pocket. But I was determined to make it work, to carve out a life for myself in this new and exciting place. And so, I set off on the long journey, driving through the night and into the early hours of the morning.

It was a long and arduous journey, but I never lost sight of my goal. I was young, full of hope and determination, and I knew that anything was possible if I just kept pushing forward.

And then, finally, I arrived. I crossed the state line into Florida, and I felt a surge of excitement coursing through my veins. I had made it. I had arrived.

Clearwater was everything I had hoped it would be, and more. The town was alive with energy and excitement, and I felt like I had finally found my place in the world. But this was short-lived.

It was supposed to be a fun weekend. My cousin invited me over to his apartment to hang out and catch up. We hadn't seen each other in a while, and I was excited to spend some time with him. Little did I know that things were about to take a turn for the worse.

After a long day of reminiscing and catching up, my cousin and I decided to smoke some weed. He had his own stash, but I had brought some of my own. I carefully measured out the amount I wanted to smoke and put it in the bowl.

As we were about to light up, my cousin's roommate walked in. He was a tall, lanky guy with shaggy hair and a laid-back demeanor. He asked if he could join us, and we said sure. I didn't think anything of it at the time, but looking back, I should have been more cautious.

The three of us sat around the coffee table, passing the bowl back and forth. I noticed that the roommate was taking bigger hits than the rest of us, but I didn't say anything. I just assumed he had a higher tolerance.

But then he did something that really pissed me off. He took the bowl and dumped the remaining weed into it, without asking anyone else if that was okay. I was shocked and angry. That was my weed, and he had just stolen it from me.

I confronted him about it, telling him that he couldn't just take my weed like that. He laughed it off and said that he was just trying to keep the party going. I didn't find it funny.

Things escalated from there. I stood up and got in his face, telling him that he needed to give me back my weed. He pushed me back, and before I knew it, we were wrestling on the floor.

It was a messy fight, with punches and kicks flying everywhere. I could hear my cousin yelling at us to stop, but I couldn't focus on anything except the guy in front of me. I was determined to get my weed back, no matter what.

In the end, I emerged victorious. I managed to pin the roommate down and retrieve my stolen weed. He stormed out of the apartment, and my cousin and I were left shaken and exhausted.

I realize that I probably overreacted. I shouldn't have let my anger get the best of me, especially since it was just a small amount of weed. But in the heat of the moment, all I could think about was getting my property back. Looking back on that time now, so many years later, I am filled with a sense of nostalgia and wonder. I realize that that journey was just the beginning, the first step on a long and winding road that would take me to places I never could have imagined.

Now, whenever I think about that weekend, I feel a mix of regret and pride. Regret for letting my emotions get the best of me, but pride for standing up for myself and not letting someone take advantage of me. It's a lesson I won't forget anytime soon.

Unfortunately, the fight with my cousin's roommate was just the beginning of my troubles. My cousin was understandably upset by the altercation, and he told me that I needed to leave his apartment and not come back.

I was stunned. I had nowhere else to go in the city, and I didn't know what to do. I begged my cousin to let me stay, but he was firm. He didn't want any more drama in his life.

So, with no other options, I called my uncle in Tennessee. He had always been a bit of a black sheep in the family. I explained my situation to him, and he agreed to let me stay with him for a while. A decision I would regret.

It was a long and lonely journey to Tennessee. I had never been to the state before, and I didn't know anyone there besides my uncle. I spent most of the trip thinking about what had gone wrong with my cousin and his roommate, and how I could have handled things differently.

When I arrived at my uncle's house, he greeted me with a warm smile and a hug. He could tell that I was upset and offered to listen to my story. I told him everything that had happened, from the fight with the roommate to my falling out with my cousin.

My uncle wasn't sympathetic, but he also gave me some tough love. He told me that I needed to take responsibility for my actions, and that I couldn't keep blaming other people for my problems. It was a harsh truth, but I knew he was right. But as you know, my uncle didn't live by these words, so it was confusing.

"Broken but not Destroyed"
Breaking a cycle...

CHAPTER 13

It wasn't always like this. Once upon a time, I was a bright kid with a bright future ahead of me. But then I got hooked on prescription painkillers, and things started to spiral out of control. Before I knew it, I was sleeping from house to house on Skid Row, using needles to inject heroin.

I was consumed by my addiction. It was all I could think about. I spent my days begging for money, scrounging for food, and trying to find my next fix. I had lost everything - my family, my friends, my job - and I knew that my future looked bleak.

But I didn't care. All I wanted was that next hit, that next rush of euphoria that would take me away from my problems. And so, I continued to use, day after day, week after week, with no end in sight.

It wasn't long before I started to do things that I never thought I would do. I started robbing drunks at the end of the night after bar closing. It was a thrill, a rush of adrenaline that temporarily took me away from my pain. But it was wrong, and I knew it. I was ashamed of myself, but I couldn't stop.

One night, I was caught in the act and arrested. I spent the next few years in jail, separated from the world I once knew. When I was finally released, I found that I had nothing left. My family had moved on without me, my friends were gone, and I was still addicted to drugs.

But something inside me had changed. I knew that I couldn't go on like this anymore. I knew that I had hit rock bottom, and that the only way to go was up. And so, I checked myself into a rehab facility, determined to turn my life around.

I was stuck in a cycle of addiction, and it was a nightmare. I went through numerous rehab facilities and had been arrested over thirteen times. I had even served time in prison. It was a never-ending cycle that I couldn't seem to break out of, and I was tired of it.

I knew that I needed to make a change, and I decided to take control of my life. I started by admitting that I had a problem and needed help. I went to meetings and talked to other addicts who had gone through similar struggles.

It wasn't easy, and there were times when I stumbled and fell back into old habits. But I kept pushing forward. I knew that I had to take responsibility for my actions and that I was the only one who could change my life.

I started to make changes in my life, both big and small. I cut ties with people who were a bad influence on me and started to surround myself with positive and supportive people. I also started to take better care of myself, both physically and mentally.

I started to rediscover the things that I loved and the things that made me happy. I found joy in simple things like going for a walk or spending time with friends. It was a slow process, but I was making progress.

It wasn't always easy, and there were times when I felt like giving up. But I knew that I couldn't go back to my old life. I had to keep moving forward, no matter how hard it was.

I've never ever wanted to be in prison again, or to be on drugs again ever again.

Today, I am proud to say that I am in recovery. I have been sobered for over 7 years, and I am living a life that I never thought was possible. I have a job that I love, with a beautiful fiancé and I am surrounded by people who support me and believe in me.

I am not saying that it was easy. It was the hardest thing that I have ever done in my life. But it was worth it. I am finally free from the cycle of addiction that had held me captive for so long.

Addiction is a difficult journey, but it is possible to break the cycle. It takes hard work, dedication, and a willingness to change. But if you keep moving forward, you can overcome your addiction and live a life that is free from the pain and suffering that comes with it.

TikTok

TikTok has become an important part of my life. It has provided me with an outlet during a time in my life where things weren't looking so good. I was homeless and my second oldest child had Covid. My oldest was embarrassed about having to go to school from a hotel, but I was doing my best to be a good father and provide for my family while staying sober. I had just gotten out of an abusive marriage, and it was a horrible experience for both me and my kids. I don't want to talk about her at all, but that experience provided me with a deep understanding of what I will tolerate, and what I will not let ever happen in my household again.

I was only homeless for a few months, as I quickly gained employment welding. My first job in production welding was in iron Mountain, and I ran a welding machine. It was CNC welding mixed, and it was a fun job. Welding has always been a passion of mine, and it felt great to be working again.

After some time, I was able to find a house for my family. It was a relief to finally have a place to call home. Despite the challenges that I faced, I remained determined to provide a better life for my children. TikTok has been a source of inspiration for me, and it has helped me to stay positive during difficult times.

Looking back, I am proud of how far I have come. I have overcome many obstacles, and I am grateful for the lessons that I have learned. My experience has taught me the importance of resilience, perseverance, and determination. I am excited to see what the future holds for me and my family.

"Broken but not Destroyed"
Meet Kat

CHAPTER 14

Living in Iron Mountain, Michigan was a unique experience for me. It was a small town, but it had its own charm and beauty. I was fortunate enough to live on a vast 10-acre land at the base of an international ski jump. The view was breathtaking, and the fresh air was invigorating. It was a perfect place to raise a family and enjoy the great outdoors.

I was thrilled to finally have a four-bedroom house to call my own. It was a significant step up from my previous living situation, and it felt like a dream come true. As a father, I was determined to be a stable and responsible parent. I worked as a welder at Boss snow plow, where I found joy in the hands-on work and the satisfaction that came with creating something from scratch.

However, as much as I enjoyed my job and my family life, I couldn't shake off the feeling of loneliness that sometimes crept in. Living in a small town had its perks, but it also meant that opportunities to connect with like-minded individuals were limited. I found myself longing for my old lifestyle, where I was immersed in a world of people from all walks of life, even if it was within the drug-addicted world.

Despite this, I knew that I wanted to make a difference in the world, and I believed that social media was the platform to do it. I started creating content online, focusing on spreading positivity and joy to anyone who came across my page. I wanted to use my platform to make people smile, to brighten up their day, and to inspire them to be their best selves.

As I continued to create content while working and raising my family, I began to develop a sense of who I was as a person. I realized that my purpose was to bring happiness to others, and it was a lot of fun. The messages and feedback that I received from people were incredibly inspirational, and they helped me stay motivated and positive every day. So thank you so much I mean[you.]!

Through my content creation, I found a way to connect with people from all over the world. I was able to inspire and uplift others, and in turn, they inspired and uplifted me. It was a beautiful cycle of positivity, and it gave me a sense of fulfillment that I had never felt before.

In the end, living in Iron Mountain, Michigan was a unique experience that taught me a lot about myself and what I wanted to achieve in life. I learned that even in the smallest of towns, there are opportunities to make a difference and connect with others. And through my journey, I found my purpose and the joy that comes with spreading positivity to others.

As I mentioned earlier, living in Iron Mountain, Michigan was a unique experience. It was a beautiful place, but I felt lonely at times, and I longed for something more. Little did I know, God had a plan for me, and it involved the most amazing woman I had ever met.

It all started with a message from Kat. She messaged me because her daughter, Ella, asked her to, just to tell me that they really liked the way I signed music. At first, I didn't think anything of it because I received thousands of messages daily. But for some reason, Kat's message stood out to me. There was something about her words that touched my heart and made me want to know more about her.

From that first message, Kat and I became friends. We talked on the phone for the first time, and it was like we had known each other forever. There was an instant connection between us, and I knew deep down that this woman was my forever.

However, I was cautious. My previous relationship had left me scarred, and I was protective of my kids. I wanted to make sure that whoever came into my life would love my children as much as I did.

So Kat would have to love my kids as her own, But I would also love Ella like my own, and without hesitation, I knew she would, and she's done so ever since.

As I got to know Kat better, I realized how truly amazing she was. She was kind, compassionate, and loving, not only to me but also to my kids. She went out of her way to make them feel special and loved, and they adored her in return.

I knew that this woman was the one for me, and I couldn't wait to spend the rest of my life with her. Kat will became my wife and my kids' stepmother. We are truly blessed to have Kat in our lives. It was the best decision I ever made, and I thank God every day for bringing her into my life.

Kat's love and support have been unwavering, and she has helped me become the best version of myself. She has been my rock through thick and thin, and I know that I can always count on her.

Looking back, I am grateful for the way God brought Kat into my life. It was unexpected, and I didn't understand it at the time, but now I see that it was all part of His divine plan. Kat is my soulmate, my best friend, and the love of my life.

When I reflect on my relationship with Kat, it hasn't always been a smooth ride. We've had our fair share of disagreements, misunderstandings, and challenges that have tested our commitment to each other. However, what I can say with confidence is that we've always approached each problem and situation with love for each other.

Being in a committed relationship with Kat has taught me the value of patience. As someone who has spent time in prison, transitioning back into society has been an uphill battle. Even though it's been years since my release, I still grapple with the emotional toll that prison took on me, particularly the PTSD. However, Kat has been a constant source of support and stability in my life.

She has learned to be a neutralizer of my episodes, helping me to navigate my triggers and manage my emotions. I don't know what I would do without her. She's been my rock, my confidant, and my partner in all aspects of life. I'm grateful for her unwavering love and commitment to me, even when things get tough.

Dealing with an ex-prisoner isn't easy, but Kat has taken it all in stride. She's had to navigate the stigma and stereotypes that come with being in a relationship with someone who has a criminal record. But she's never once judged me or made me feel like less of a person because of my past mistakes.

Instead, she's helped me to become the best version of myself. She's encouraged me to pursue my dreams and aspirations, even when they seemed impossible. She's believed in me when I didn't believe in myself, and for that, I will always be grateful.

I know that I'm not perfect, and I've made my fair share of mistakes. But with Kat by my side, I feel like I can face anything that comes my way. She's taught me the importance of communication, forgiveness, and understanding in a relationship. We've learned to listen to each other, respect each other's boundaries, and work through our issues as a team.

In many ways, Kat and I are like two puzzle pieces that fit perfectly together. We complement each other's strengths and weaknesses, and we bring out the best in each other. Our relationship isn't perfect, but it's real, and it's built on a foundation of love and respect.

As I look to the future, I know that there will be more challenges and obstacles to overcome. But with Kat by my side, I feel like I can face anything that comes my way. She's my partner, my best friend, and the love of my life. And for that, I will always be grateful.

"Broken, but not Destroyed"
The big move

Chapter 15

Leaving behind the familiar life in Iron Mountain, Michigan was a monumental decision for me. It was a decision that would alter the course of my life forever. After much contemplation and soul-searching, I decided to make my way down south. And, boy, was it the second-best decision I ever made in my life!

The prospect of adventure and new beginnings was exhilarating. I was leaving behind a life that had become monotonous and stagnant. The thought of starting afresh was liberating. I was excited about the endless possibilities that lay ahead. The journey to my destination was long and arduous, but I knew it was worth it.

When I arrived in North Carolina, I moved in with Kat. She encouraging me to make the move. As soon as I stepped into her apartment, I felt like I was home. It was a small two-bedroom apartment, but it was cozy and welcoming. The walls were adorned with pictures and the color teal everywhere giving it a homie touch. The smell of freshly brewed coffee wafted through the air, making me feel instantly at ease.

Kat and Ella. Ella who was just a few years younger than my youngest son. She was a bubbly and vivacious little girl who welcomed us with open arms. My boys were excited to meet her, and they hit it off right away. The apartment suddenly felt smaller with the addition of three rambunctious boys, but we made it work. We rearranged the furniture, and created a space that felt like our own.

Leaving behind the stigma and lifestyle that surrounded Iron Michigan, was a significant relief. The constant pressure to conform to societal norms and expectations had taken a toll on my mental and emotional well-being. I was tired of living a life that felt like a never-ending cycle of hurt and pain.

Moving to a new place gave me a new hope. It was a chance to start over and create a life that was fulfilling and meaningful.

The first few weeks in North Carolina were challenging. I had to adjust to a new environment, new people, and new customs. It was overwhelming at times, but I persevered. I learned that the true battle in life is when we battle ourselves. The victories are when we win those battles against ourselves. I had to confront my fears, doubts, and insecurities. It was a painful process, but it was necessary for my growth.

Kat was a constant source of support and encouragement. She helped me navigate the challenges of starting over in a new place. She introduced me to her friends, took me to local events, and showed me around town. I felt like I had a community of people who cared about me and my well-being.

Moving to North Carolina was not an easy decision, but it was one of the best decisions I ever made. It gave me a chance to create a life that I was proud of. It taught me that sometimes you have to leave behind the familiar to find your true calling. It gave me a sense of purpose and direction that I had been missing for a long time. And most importantly, it brought me closer to the people I love.

As a person who had lived in the north for most of my life, moving down south was a significant cultural shock to me. The people in the south were different from what I was used to. They were more inviting, friendly, and accommodating. It was a new experience for me, and I had to adjust to this new way of life. And I've learned that the phrase bless it. Can me and good or bad.

On the other hand, the people in the north were a no-nonsense kind of people. They were direct, hands-on, and said it as it is. This was in contrast to the people down south, who were more polite and courteous. It took me some time to get used to this new culture, but I eventually adapted to it.

One of the first battles that I faced was going into the store. I would often feel overwhelmed with crowds, and my body would instantly break out in sweat. It was a new experience for me, and I had to learn how to cope with it. I would take deep breaths and remind myself that it was just a store, and there was nothing to be afraid of. Over time, I developed coping mechanisms that helped me deal with these overwhelming situations.

Despite the challenges, I knew that being in North Carolina was the right decision for me. It was an opportunity to be out of my comfort zone and experience new things. It was a chance to grow and learn more about myself. I knew that if I went back to Michigan every other week, I would be missing out on all the beautiful things that North Carolina had to offer.

I learned to embrace the beauty in each battle that I faced. Every time I overcame a challenge, it made me stronger and more resilient. I learned that life is full of battles, and it is up to us to decide how we respond to them.

Living in North Carolina was a transformational experience for me. It taught me to be more open-minded, accepting, and accommodating. I learned that people from different parts of the country have different ways of life, and that is okay. It taught me to appreciate the differences that make us unique.

The beauty of North Carolina was not just in its people. It was in the scenic beauty that surrounded me. The lush green forests, the rolling hills, and the beautiful beaches were a sight to behold. It was a reminder that there is so much beauty in the world if we just take the time to appreciate it.

My move from the north to the south was a significant decision that changed my life forever. It was a chance to experience a new way of life and embrace the beauty of the world. It was a reminder that life is full of battles, but it is up to us to decide how we respond to them. I am grateful for this experience.

Now, I am more than open to opportunity. I take comfort in knowing that the Horizon is only a new experience, and your current situation can be changed with preparation action we can choose to stand still. Or take action and be the change.

Perception is a powerful force that shapes our experiences and influences our actions. It is the lens through which we view the world, and it can color our thoughts, emotions, and behaviors. Our perceptions are influenced by a variety of factors, including our upbringing, culture, education, and past experiences.

When we see the world in a positive light, we are more likely to have positive experiences and outcomes. Conversely, when we view the world negatively, we are more likely to have negative experiences and outcomes. This is because our perceptions shape our thoughts and emotions, which in turn influence our behaviors and actions.

Changing your perception can be challenging, but it is essential if you want to improve your life. It requires a shift in your thought process, a willingness to challenge your assumptions and beliefs, and a commitment to adopting new ways of thinking.

One way to change your perception is to focus on the positive aspects of your life and the world around you. Instead of dwelling on the negative, try to find the good in every situation. This can help you cultivate a more optimistic outlook and improve your overall well-being.

Another way to change your perception is to practice mindfulness. Mindfulness involves paying attention to the present moment without judgment. By being fully present and aware, you can better understand your thoughts and emotions and gain greater control over your reactions.

It is also helpful to surround yourself with positive influences, such as supportive friends and family members, inspiring role models, and uplifting media. By being around people and things that uplift and inspire you, you can cultivate a more positive outlook and improve your overall quality of life.

Perception is a powerful force that can shape our experiences and outcomes. By changing our perceptions, we can change our thoughts, emotions, and behaviors, and ultimately improve our lives. It requires a willingness to challenge our assumptions and beliefs, a commitment to adopting new ways of thinking, and a focus on the positive aspects of our lives and the world around us.

"Broken but not Destroyed"
Walk what we talk...

CHAPTER 16

I have been through a lot in my life, and while my experiences have been challenging, they have taught me invaluable lessons about myself and about life. One of the most significant obstacles I faced was my drug addiction, which eventually led to a prison sentence. However, in hindsight, I can see that these experiences were essential in shaping who I am today.

Overcoming addiction is never easy. It requires a tremendous amount of strength, determination, and the willingness to seek help. For me, it took hitting rock bottom before I realized that I needed to make a change. It wasn't just about getting clean; I had to learn how to live a life free of drugs. I had to learn how to cope with my emotions and the challenges that life throws our way without turning to substances.

Going through a prison sentence was tough, but it was also a time of introspection and self-reflection. I had to learn how to become a man all over again, but this time, without the crutch of drugs. It wasn't easy, but it was necessary. During this time, I learned the importance of resilience and perseverance. I realized that even in the most challenging of circumstances, we have the power to choose how we respond. I chose to use my time in prison to better myself, to learn from my mistakes, and to prepare for a better future.

When I was released from prison, I knew that I had to create a life for myself that was stable and safe. I needed a place to call home and a supportive community. I was blessed to have both. Finding a job wasn't easy, but I persisted, and eventually, I landed a position that allowed me to support myself financially. Having a stable income and a home to go to each day gave me a sense of purpose and belonging.

As I settled into my new life, I began to focus on my personal growth. I read books on self-improvement. Through these experiences, I learned the importance of self-care and self-love. I realized that in order to be the best version of myself, I had to prioritize my mental and emotional well-being.

While my journey hasn't been perfect, I'm proud of the progress I've made thus far. I'm grateful for the blessings that God has bestowed upon me, including my family and my home. They have been a source of love and support that I never knew I needed. Having a stable environment has allowed me to focus on my personal growth and to work through my problems in a healthy way.

I know that my journey is far from over, and that personal growth is an ongoing process. However, I'm committed to becoming the best version of myself that I can be. I want to continue to learn, to grow, and to inspire others who may be going through similar struggles. I believe that our experiences, no matter how challenging, can ultimately be used for good. My story is a testament to that.

I'm telling you all of this to recap my life to show you that my life is no different than anybody that has been faced with struggles in diversity's. Your struggles may have been different from mine, but they all produced the same type of pain. this pain is beautiful. It is a reminder that we must keep on pushing, and that in the midst of all that pain, we are learning lessons that we will never understand.

My experiences with addiction and incarceration were difficult, but they taught me valuable life lessons. Through perseverance, resilience, and a commitment to personal growth, I was able to overcome these challenges and create a life for myself that I'm proud of. I'm grateful for the blessings that God has bestowed upon me, and I'm committed to using my experiences to help others who may be struggling.

As I reflect on my life and all that I have been through, I am filled with a deep sense of gratitude for all the blessings that God has bestowed upon me. I am reminded that every trial and tribulation that I faced was only possible to overcome because of God's unwavering love and support.

Throughout my journey, I have learned that God never abandons us, even in our darkest moments. He is always there, guiding us and giving us the strength to keep moving forward. It is through our faith in Him that we can overcome any obstacle and emerge stronger on the other side.

My story is a testament to this truth. I have faced many challenges in my life, from personal struggles to professional setbacks. But every time I found myself at a crossroads, God was there to show me the way. Through His divine intervention, I was able to overcome my fears and doubts and achieve my goals.

In sharing my story, I hope to inspire others to have faith in God and trust in His plan for their lives. No matter what you are going through, know that God is with you, and He will never leave your side.

With His help, you can overcome any challenge and achieve your dreams.

I encourage you to take a moment to reflect on all the blessings in your life and give thanks to God for His love and guidance. Remember that every obstacle you face is an opportunity to grow in faith and become a stronger, more resilient person.

In closing, I want to remind you that God's love is infinite and unconditional. He is always there, waiting for us to turn to Him and seek His guidance. So, no matter what you are going through, know that you are never alone, and with God's help, you can overcome anything. Trust in His plan for your life, and you will see that the possibilities are endless.

More Books from Author:

Anthony Eagle Jr.

The Devil Was An Angel, Too

I'm Everyone's Problem

Available Now!!

www.chrimsan.com

www.ingramcontent.com/pod-product-compliance
Lightning Source LLC
Chambersburg PA
CBHW071412300426
44114CB00016B/2280